Furniture
for 5- & 10-Inch Dolls™

p. 6

p. 2

p. 19

p. 14

p. 30

p. 25

p. 56

p. 43

p. 51

p. 38

5-Inch Doll Rocking Chair

Size: 5¼ inches W x 5¾ inches H x 4⅜ inches D
(13.3cm x 14.6cm x 11.1cm)
Skill Level: Advanced

Materials

❏ 1 artist-style sheet 7-count plastic canvas
❏ Red Heart Super Saver Art. E300 medium weight
yarn as listed in color key
❏ #16 tapestry needle

Cutting & Stitching

1 Cut plastic canvas according to graphs (pages 3–5). Base (C) will remain unstitched.

2 Stitch remaining pieces following graphs, overlapping one hole on seat cushion (J) where indicated on graph and stitching together as shown, creating a tube. Work only area shown on back frame (I).

3 Using Aspen print, Overcast side edges on back (B) between arrow and red star.

Assembly

Note: Follow graphs and assembly diagram throughout assembly.

1 Using Aspen print, Whipstitch unstitched base (C) to front frame (H) along bottom edge. Using buff, Whipstitch top edges of rocker sides (F) between brackets to underneath side of base (C) where indicated with red lines. *Note: Make sure back sides of each pair of rocker sides (F) are facing each other so right sides face out.*

2 Use Aspen print through step 6. Whipstitch back band (M) to back (A) around side and top edges from arrow to arrow, easing as necessary to fit. Whipstitch back band (N) to back (A) along bottom edge. Whipstitch back bands (M) and (N) together. Whipstitch back band (M) to back (B) around sides and top from arrow to arrow.

3 Whipstitch 19-hole edges of the following pieces together in this order, forming one long piece: one side (L), one arm (E), cushion seat support (D), one arm (E) and one side (L).

4 Whipstitch cushion seat support (D) to top middle edge of front frame (H) where indicated. Whipstitch sides (L) to front frame (H) and to base (C). Whipstitch arms (E) to remaining edges of front frame (H), easing as necessary to fit.

5 Whipstitch back frame (I) to sides (L) and arms (E), easing as necessary to fit. Whipstitch remaining edges of arms (E) and cushion seat support (D) to back frame (I) along bars indicated with red lines.

6 Slide assembled chair back (A, B and M) over back frame (I); Whipstitch back (B) to sides (L) and back frame (I) and to base (C), working through all three layers along side edges. *Note: Because back (B) is one hole smaller, it will be centered over back frame (I) and Whipstitches will be longer.*

7 Using buff, Whipstitch rockers (G) to rocker sides (F) around remaining edges.

8 Using Aspen print and with seam of seat cushion (J) at center bottom, flatten tube enough so seat cushion sides (K) will fit into space created; Whipstitch in place, easing as necessary to fit. Place cushion in chair.

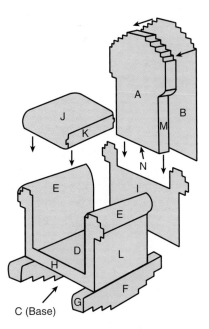

5-Inch Doll Rocking Chair
Assembly Diagram

Back (A)
24 holes x 28 holes
Cut 1

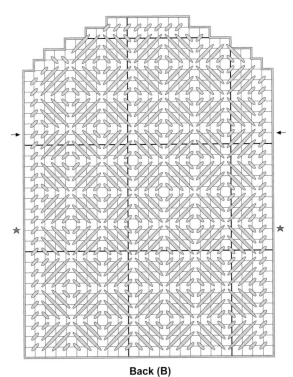

Back (B)
24 holes x 32 holes
Cut 1

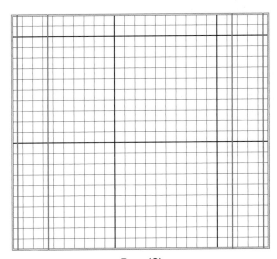

Base (C)
25 holes x 22 holes
Cut 1
Do not stitch

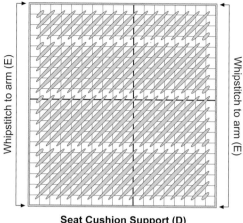

Seat Cushion Support (D)
18 holes x 19 holes
Cut 1

Arm (E)
19 holes x 25 holes
Cut 2

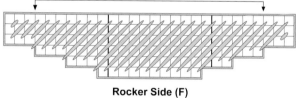

Rocker Side (F)
28 holes x 6 holes
Cut 4

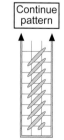

Rocker (G)
3 holes x 41 holes
Cut 2

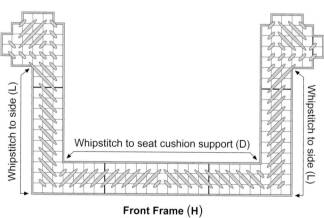

Front Frame (H)
31 holes x 17 holes
Cut 1

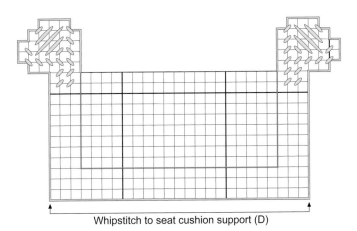

Whipstitch to seat cushion support (D)

Back Frame (I)
31 holes x 17 holes
Cut 1

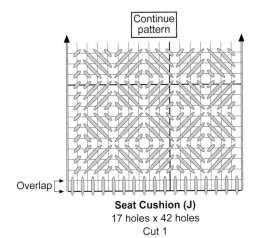

Continue pattern

Overlap

Seat Cushion (J)
17 holes x 42 holes
Cut 1

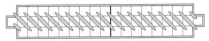

Seat Cushion Side (K)
19 holes x 3 holes
Cut 2

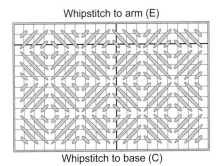

Whipstitch to arm (E)

Whipstitch to base (C)

Side (L)
19 holes x 12 holes
Cut 2

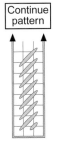

Continue pattern

Back Band (M)
3 holes x 72 holes
Cut 1

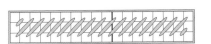

Back Band (N)
18 holes x 3 holes
Cut 1

10-Inch Doll Rocking Chair

Size: 8¾ inches W x 11 inches H x 8⅜ inches D
(22.2cm x 27.9cm x 21.3cm)
Skill Level: Advanced

Materials

❏ 2 artist-style sheets 7-count plastic canvas
❏ Red Heart Super Saver Art. E300 medium weight yarn as listed in color key
❏ #16 tapestry needle
❏ Stuffing material (sample used plastic foam packing peanuts)

Cutting & Stitching

1 Cut plastic canvas according to graphs (pages 7–13).

2 Stitch pieces following graphs, overlapping one hole on seat cushion (J) where indicated on graph and stitching together as shown, creating a tube. Work only area shown on back frame (I).

3 Using Aspen print, Overcast side edges on back (B) between arrow and red star.

Assembly

Note: Follow graphs and assembly diagram throughout assembly.

1 Using Aspen print, Whipstitch front and back aprons (O) to side aprons (P). Whipstitch base (C) to bottom edges of assembled apron.

2 Using buff through step 3, Whipstitch top edges of rocker sides (F) between brackets to underneath side of base (C) where indicated with red lines. *Note: Make sure back sides of each pair of rocker sides (F) are facing each other so right sides face out.*

3 Whipstitch rockers (G) to rocker sides (F) around remaining edges, filling with stuffing material for support before closing.

4 Use Aspen print through step 10. Whipstitch back band (M) to back (A) around side and top edges from arrow to arrow, easing as necessary to fit. Whipstitch back band (N) to back (A) along bottom edge. Whipstitch back bands (M) and (N) together. Whipstitch back band (M) to back (B) around sides and top from arrow to arrow.

5 Whipstitch 38-hole edges of the following pieces together in this order, forming one long piece: one

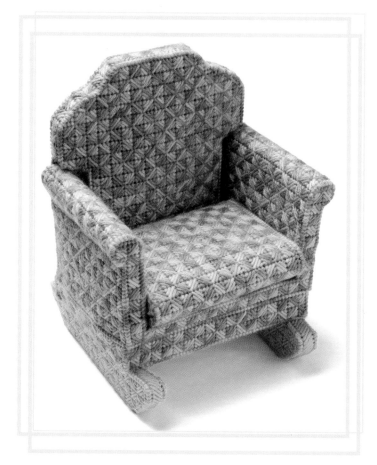

side (L), one arm (E), cushion seat support (D), one arm (E) and one side (L).

6 Whipstitch cushion seat support (D) to top middle edge of front frame (H) where indicated. Whipstitch sides (L) to front frame (H). Whipstitch arms (E) to remaining edges of front frame (H), easing as necessary to fit.

7 Whipstitch back frame (I) to sides (L) and arms (E), easing as necessary to fit. Whipstitch remaining edges of arms (E) to back frame (I) along bars indicated with red lines.

8 Slide assembled chair back (A, B and M) over back frame (I); Whipstitch back (B) to sides (L) and to back frame (I), working through all three layers and inserting stuffing material between back (A) and back frame (I)

9 Whipstitch assembled top part of chair to top edges of apron pieces (O and P), filling chair with stuffing material before closing.

10 With seam of seat cushion (J) at center bottom, flatten tube enough so seat cushion sides (K) will fit into space created; Whipstitch in place, easing as necessary to fit and filling with stuffing material before closing. Place cushion in chair.

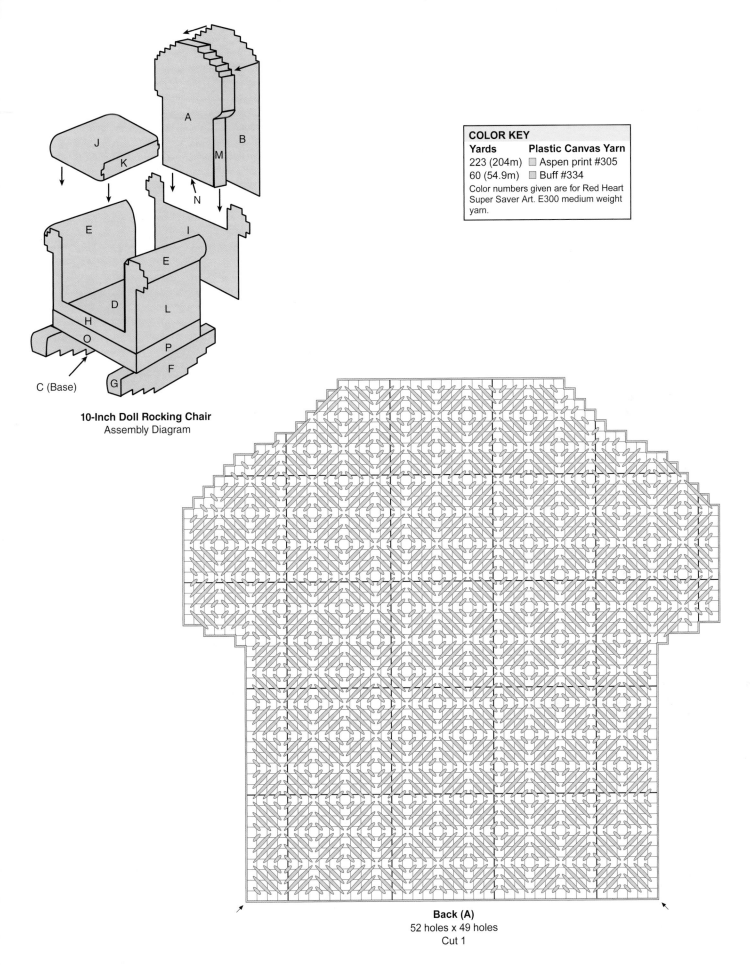

10-Inch Doll Rocking Chair
Assembly Diagram

C (Base)

COLOR KEY

Yards	Plastic Canvas Yarn
223 (204m)	☐ Aspen print #305
60 (54.9m)	☐ Buff #334

Color numbers given are for Red Heart Super Saver Art. E300 medium weight yarn.

Back (A)
52 holes x 49 holes
Cut 1

Back (B)
52 holes x 55 holes
Cut 1

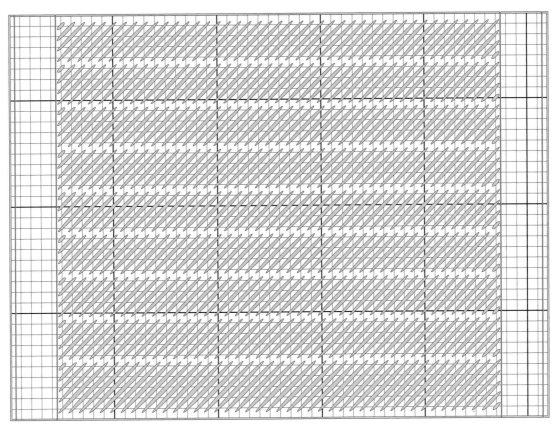

Base (C)
52 holes x 38 holes
Cut 1

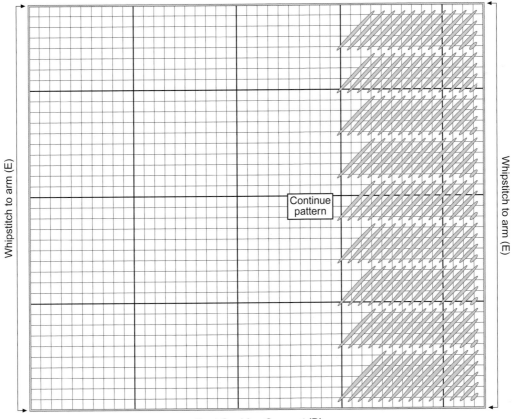

Whipstitch to arm (E)

Whipstitch to arm (E)

Continue pattern

Seat Cushion Support (D)
44 holes x 38 holes
Cut 1
May leave unstitched if desired

COLOR KEY

Yards	Plastic Canvas Yarn
223 (204m)	☐ Aspen print #305
60 (54.9m)	☐ Buff #334

Color numbers given are for Red Heart
Super Saver Art. E300 medium weight
yarn.

Whipstitch to upper side (L)

Whipstitch to seat cushion support (D)

Arm (E)
38 holes x 38 holes
Cut 2

Whipstitch to base (C)

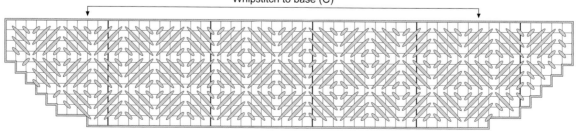

Rocker Side (F)
55 holes x 10 holes
Cut 4

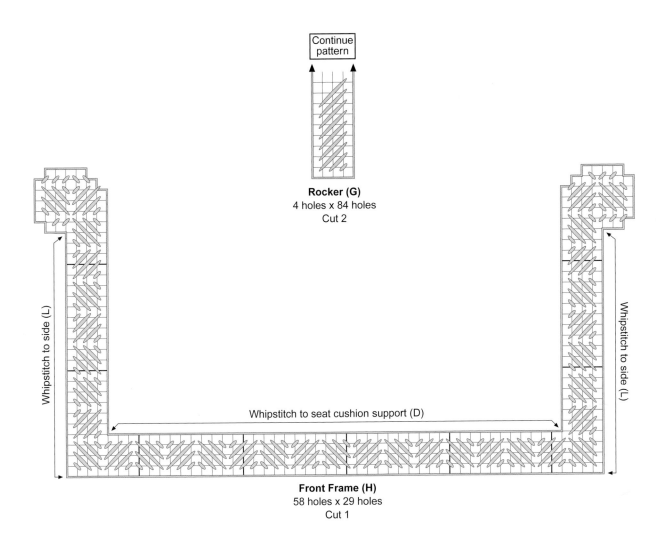

Continue pattern

Rocker (G)
4 holes x 84 holes
Cut 2

Whipstitch to side (L)

Whipstitch to side (L)

Whipstitch to seat cushion support (D)

Front Frame (H)
58 holes x 29 holes
Cut 1

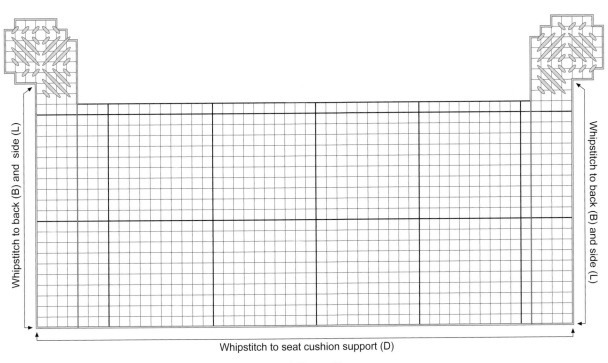

Whipstitch to back (B) and side (L)

Whipstitch to back (B) and side (L)

Whipstitch to seat cushion support (D)

Back Frame (I)
58 holes x 29 holes
Cut 1

Continue
pattern

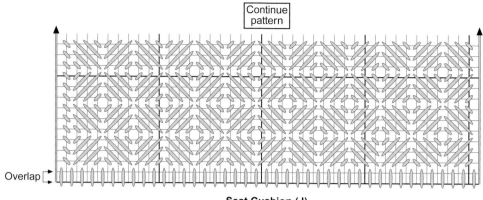

Overlap

Seat Cushion (J)
41 holes x 77 holes
Cut 1

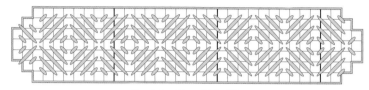

Seat Cushion Side (K)
34 holes x 7 holes
Cut 2

Whipstitch to arm (E)

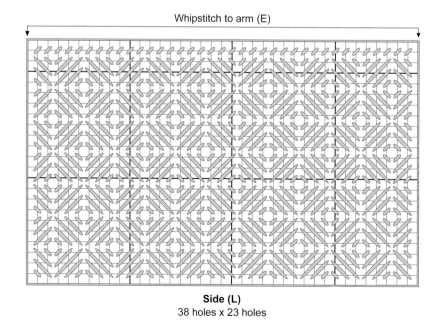

Side (L)
38 holes x 23 holes
Cut 2

Continue pattern

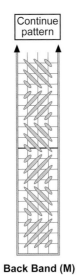

Back Band (M)
4 holes x 138 holes
Cut 1

Continue pattern

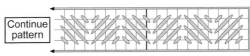

Back Band (N)
40 holes x 4 holes
Cut 1

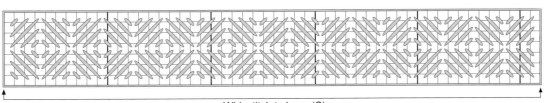

Whipstitch to base (C)

Front & Back Apron (O)
52 holes x 7 holes
Cut 2

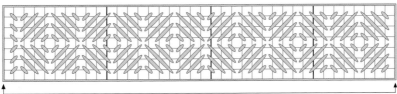

Whipstitch to base (C)

Side Apron (P)
38 holes x 7 holes
Cut 2

5-Inch Doll Car Seat

Size: 5 inches W x 7½ inches L x 9 inches H
(12.7cm x 19cm x 22.9cm), including handle
Skill Level: Advanced

Materials

- ❑ 1 artist-style sheet clear 7-count plastic canvas
- ❑ Small amount ivory 7-count plastic canvas
- ❑ Red Heart Super Saver Art. E300 medium weight yarn as listed in color key
- ❑ 6-strand embroidery floss as listed in color key
- ❑ #16 tapestry needle
- ❑ Crewel/embroidery needle with large eye
- ❑ Hand-sewing needle
- ❑ Sewing thread: green to match yarn and white
- ❑ 8 x 12-inch (20.3 x 30.5cm) piece coordinating fabric (sample used brown with ivory polka dots)
- ❑ 4 (⅝-inch/15mm) brown toned buttons
- ❑ ⅔ yard (0.6m) ½-inch/12mm-wide brown grosgrain ribbon
- ❑ ¾ inch (1.9cm) ½-inch/1.3cm-wide hook-and-loop tape
- ❑ Stuffing material (sample used plastic foam packing peanuts)
- ❑ Fabric glue

Project Note

Follow graphs and assembly diagrams throughout.

Cutting & Stitching

1 Cut harness (E), shoulder strap brace (F) and buckle and buckle brace (G) from ivory plastic canvas according to graphs (page 18), cutting out holes where indicated. These pieces will remain unstitched.

2 Cut all remaining pieces from clear plastic canvas according to graphs (pages 16–18), cutting out holes in seat (A).

3 Stitch pieces following graphs, working tea green stitches on seat (A) and seat sides (B) first, then working lemon stitches. Reverse one seat side (B) and one shell side (D) before stitching. *Note: Stitch only areas shown on seat sides (B).*

4 Overcast cutout holes on seat (A) with lemon. Using tea green, Overcast head edge of seat (A) and top edges of seat sides (B) from blue dot to blue dot.

5 Using buff, Overcast top edges of shell sides (D) from blue dot to blue dot and head edges of shell base (C) from blue dot to blue dot. Overcast hood band pieces (I and J).

Seat Belt Assembly

1 Cut ribbon into one 6-inch (15.2cm) length and one 14-inch (35.6cm) length.

2 For shoulder straps, thread ends of 14-inch (35.6cm) length ribbon up through holes 1 on harness (E) and down through holes 2. Pull ribbon through, leaving about a 2-inch (5.2cm) loop.

3 Thread ends through two shoulder strap holes near head edge of seat (A). Place shoulder strap brace (F) behind shoulder strap holes on seat (A) and thread through holes 1 and 2 following step 2. Pull ribbon through, measuring with doll for correct fit. *Note: Sample has 2¼–2½ inches (5.7–6.4cm) between harness (E) and shoulder strap holes.*

4 Using hand-sewing needle and green thread, sew ribbon to shoulder strap brace (F). Using a Running Stitch (page 15), sew brace (F) to seat (A) around shoulder strap hole edges.

5 For adjuster strap, thread one end of 6-inch (15.2cm) length of ribbon through buckle brace (G), coming up through hole 1 and going down through hole 2; sew ribbon in place.

6 Thread other end of ribbon up through bottom hole of seat (A), then up through hole 1 of buckle (G) and down through hole 2. Fold ribbon down on back side of buckle (G) and sew to one side of hook-and-loop tape and to buckle (G). Trim excess ribbon if needed. Using white thread, sew other side of hook-and-loop tape to seat where indicated with gray shading.

7 To fasten, bring adjuster strap up through loop below harness on shoulder straps and fasten hook-and-loop tape pieces together.

Hood Assembly

1 Lay one hood band (I) down with back side faceup. Apply a small amount of glue in area shaded with blue along length of band. For canopy, with wrong side faceup, place the 12-inch (30.5cm) edge of fabric down over glue. Place one hood band (J) centered over hood band (I). Allow to dry.

2 Using green floss and crewel/embroidery needle, work Running Stitches along long edges of hood bands (I and J).

3 Repeat steps 1 and 2 with remaining hood bands (I and J) about halfway down fabric.

4 Run a gathering stitch along edge of fabric between bands bringing middle band close to first band. Run a gathering stitch along remaining 12-inch (30.5cm) edge. Set aside.

Car Seat Assembly

1 Using tea green and with right sides facing, Whipstitch side edges of seat (A) to seat sides (B) where indicated with red lines, easing as necessary to fit and making sure to match head and foot edges.

2 Using buff, Whipstitch wrong sides of handle pieces (H) together. Place ends of handle on outside of seat sides (B) where indicated with buff triangles; tack in place with tea green.

3 Using buff, Whipstitch top edges of seat sides (B) to top edges of shell sides (D) between green star and blue dot.

4 Place ends of front and middle hood bands between seat sides (B) and shell sides (D) just in front of handle. For each side, place one button on outside and one on inside with hood band ends between. Using green floss, sew buttons in place with band ends (I and J) between, securing canopy.

5 Tuck canopy between seat side (B) and shell side (D) and behind head edge of seat (A), adjusting gathering as desired. Using crewel/embroidery needle, green floss and Running Stitch, sew sides together where indicated, working through canopy.

6 Using buff, Whipstitch side edges of shell base (C) to shell sides (D) from red arrow to red star, catching edges of seat sides (B) between yellow and red stars.

7 Using crewel/embroidery needle, green floss and Running Stitch, sew head edges of seat (A) and shell base (C) together with a Running Stitch, working through canopy.

8 Using buff and easing as necessary to fit, Whipstitch remaining edges of shell base (C) to shell sides (D), catching edges of seat side (B) in Whipstitching from green arrow to green star and filling bottom with stuffing material before closing. *Note: Foam packing peanuts will fit better if cut in smaller pieces before using.*

Running Stitch

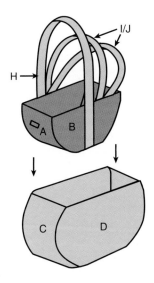

5-Inch Doll Car Seat
Assembly Diagram

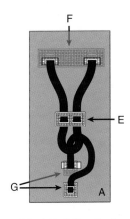

5-Inch Doll Car Seat
Seat Belt Assembly Diagram

Seat (A)
25 holes x 51 holes
Cut 1 from clear

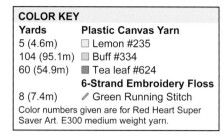
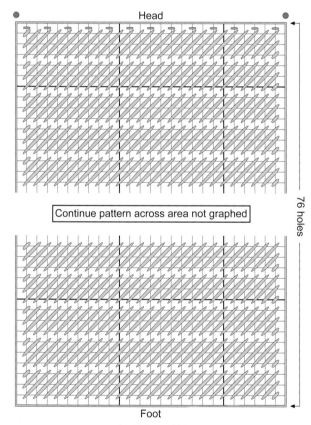

Continue pattern across area not graphed

76 holes

Shell Base (C)
26 holes x 76 holes
Cut 1 from clear

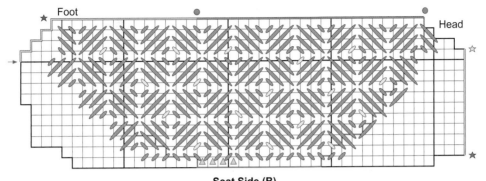

Seat Side (B)
43 holes x 14 holes
Cut 2 from clear, reverse 1

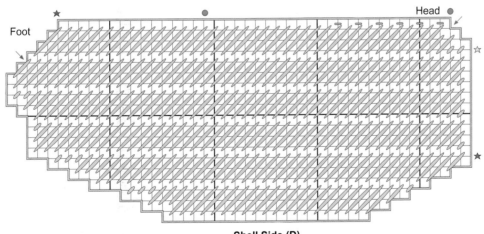

Shell Side (D)
45 holes x 19 holes
Cut 2 from clear, reverse 1

COLOR KEY	
Yards	**Plastic Canvas Yarn**
5 (4.6m)	☐ Lemon #235
104 (95.1m)	☐ Buff #334
60 (54.9m)	■ Tea leaf #624
	6-Strand Embroidery Floss
8 (7.4m)	✎ Green Running Stitch

Color numbers given are for Red Heart Super Saver Art. E300 medium weight yarn.

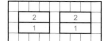

Harness (E)
9 holes x 4 holes
Cut 1 from ivory
Do not stitch

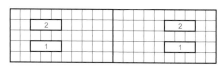

Shoulder Strap Brace (F)
20 holes x 5 holes
Cut 1 from ivory
Do not stitch

Buckle & Buckle Brace (G)
4 holes x 4 holes
Cut 2 from ivory
Do not stitch

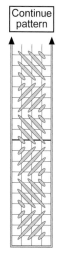

Handle (H)
4 holes x 129 holes
Cut 2 from clear

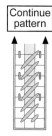

Hood Band (I)
3 holes x 80 holes
Cut 2 from clear

Hood Band (J)
3 holes x 76 holes
Cut 2 from clear

10-Inch Doll Car Seat

Size: 9 inches W x 12¾ inches L x 13¼ inches H (22.9cm x 32.4cm x 33.7cm), including handle
Skill Level: Advanced

Materials

❑ 3 artist-style sheets clear 7-count plastic canvas
❑ Red Heart Super Saver Art. E300 medium weight yarn as listed in color key
❑ 6-strand embroidery floss as listed in color key
❑ #16 tapestry needle
❑ Crewel/embroidery needle with large eye
❑ Hand-sewing needle
❑ White sewing thread
❑ 11 x 21-inch (27.9 x 53.3cm) piece coordinating fabric (sample used brown with ivory polka dots)
❑ 4 (1-inch/25.4mm) brown buttons
❑ ¾ yard (0.7m) ½-inch/12mm-wide brown grosgrain ribbon
❑ ¾ inch (1.9cm) ½-inch/1.3cm-wide hook-and-loop tape
❑ Stuffing material (sample used plastic foam packing peanuts)
❑ Fabric glue

Project Note
Follow graphs and assembly diagrams throughout.

Cutting & Stitching

1 Cut plastic canvas according to graphs (pages 21–24), cutting out holes in seat (A), harness (E), shoulder strap brace (F) and buckles (G).

2 Stitch pieces following graphs, reversing one seat side (B) and one shell side (D) before stitching. *Note: First Scotch Stitch on handles (H) is worked over 5 bars; remaining Scotch Stitches are worked over 6 bars.*

3 Overcast holes on seat (A), harness (E), shoulder strap brace (F) and buckles (G) with lemon. Using tea green, Overcast head edges of seat (A) and top edges of seat sides (B) from blue dot to blue dot.

4 Using buff throughout, Overcast top edges of shell sides (D) from blue dot to blue dot. Overcast head edge of shell base (C) from blue dot to blue dot. Overcast foot edge of shell base (C) on both sides from arrow to blue dot. Overcast hood band pieces (I and J).

Seat Belt Assembly

1 Cut ribbon into one 6-inch (15.2cm) length and one 18-inch (45.7cm) length.

2 For shoulder straps, thread ends of 18-inch (45.7cm) length of ribbon up through holes 1 on harness (E) and down through holes 2. Pull ribbon through, leaving about a 2-inch loop.

3 Thread ends through two shoulder strap holes near head edge of seat (A). Place shoulder strap brace (F) behind shoulder strap holes on seat and thread through holes 1 and 2 following step 2. Pull ribbon through, measuring with doll for correct fit. *Note: Sample has approximately 5 inches (1cm) between harness (E) and shoulder strap holes.*

4 Using hand-sewing needle and brown thread, sew ribbon to shoulder strap brace (F). Using a Running Stitch (page 20) and lemon yarn, sew brace (F) to seat (A) around shoulder strap hole edges.

5 For adjuster strap, thread one end of 6-inch (15.2cm) length of ribbon through buckle brace (G), coming up through hole 1 and going down through hole 2; fold down about 1 inch (2.5cm) on back side and sew ribbon in place.

6 Thread other end of ribbon up through bottom hole of seat (A), then up through hole 1 of buckle (G) and down through hole 2. Fold ribbon down on back side of buckle and sew to one side of hook-and-loop tape and to buckle. Trim excess ribbon if needed. Using white thread, sew other side of hook-and-loop tape to seat where indicated with gray shading.

7 To fasten, bring adjuster strap up through loop below harness on shoulder straps and fasten hook-and-loop tape pieces together.

Hood Assembly

1 Lay one hood band (I) down with back side faceup. Apply a small amount of glue in area shaded with blue along length of band. For canopy, with wrong side faceup, place the 21-inch (53.3cm) edge of fabric down over glue. Place one hood band (J) centered over hood band (I). Allow to dry.

2 Using green floss and crewel/embroidery needle, work Running Stitches along long edges of hood bands (I and J).

3 Repeat steps 1 and 2 with remaining hood bands (I and J) about halfway down fabric.

4 Run a gathering stitch along edge of fabric between bands bringing middle band close to first band. Run a gathering stitch along remaining 21-inch (53.3cm) edge. Set aside.

Car Seat Assembly

1 Using tea green and with right sides facing, Whipstitch side edges of seat (A) to seat sides (B) where indicated with red lines, easing as necessary to fit and making sure to match head and foot edges.

2 Using buff, Whipstitch wrong sides of handle pieces (H) together. Place ends of handle on outside of seat sides (B) where indicated with red lines; tack in place with tea green Running Stitch.

3 Attach seat sides (B) to shell sides (D) from green arrow to green arrow with green floss and a Running Stitch. Work a buff Running Stitch to secure shell side (D) to handle where indicated.

4 Place ends of front and middle hood bands between seat sides (B) and shell sides (D) just in front of handle. For each side, place one button on outside and one on inside with hood band ends between. Using buff, sew buttons in place with band ends (I and J) between, securing canopy.

5 Tuck canopy between seat side (B) and shell side (D) and behind head edge of seat (A), adjusting gathering as desired. Using crewel/embroidery needle,

green floss and Running Stitch, sew sides together where indicated, working through canopy.

6 Using buff, Whipstitch side edges of shell base (C) to shell sides (D) at head end from blue dot to red star.

7 Using crewel/embroidery needle, green floss and Running Stitch, sew head edges of seat (A) and shell base (C) together with a Running Stitch, working through canopy.

8 Using buff and easing as necessary to fit, Whipstitch remaining edges of shell base (C) to shell sides (D), Whipstitching from red star to blue dot at foot end and filling bottom with stuffing material before closing.

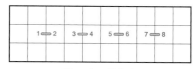

Running Stitch

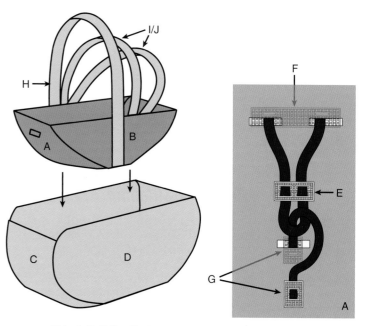

10-Inch Doll Car Seat
Assembly Diagram

10-Inch Doll Car Seat
Seat Belt Assembly Diagram

COLOR KEY		
Yards		**Plastic Canvas Yarn**
10 (9.2m)	□	Lemon #235
106 (97m)	▨	Buff #334
75 (68.6m)	▨	Tea leaf #624
	⁄	Lemon #235 Running Stitch
	⁄	Buff #334 Running Stitch
6-Strand Embroidery Floss		
12 (11m)	⁄	Green Running Stitch
Color numbers given are for Red Heart Super Saver Art. E300 medium weight yarn.		

Head

Cut out

Cut out

Continue pattern across area not graphed

Cut out

Foot

90 holes

Seat (A)
49 holes x 90 holes
Cut 1

Head

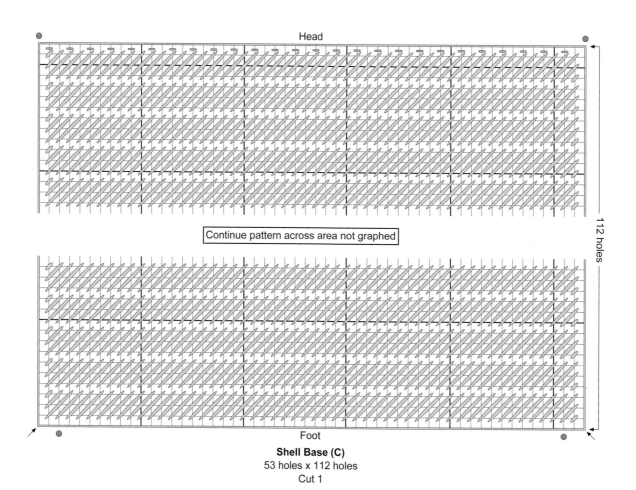

112 holes

Continue pattern across area not graphed

Foot

Shell Base (C)
53 holes x 112 holes
Cut 1

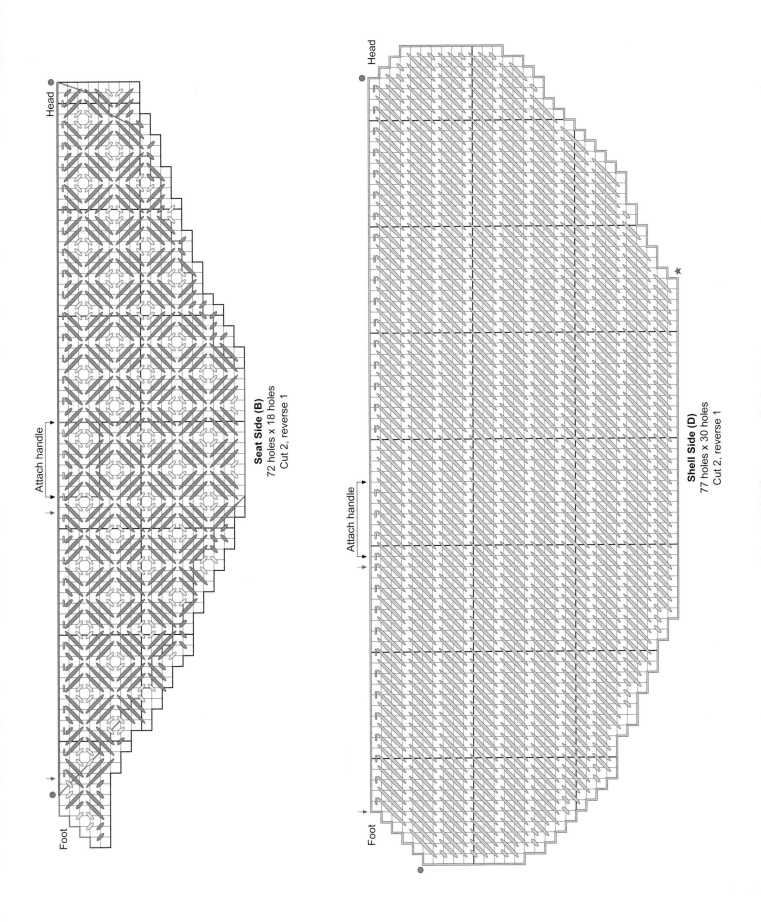

Head

Attach handle

Seat Side (B)
72 holes x 18 holes
Cut 2, reverse 1

Foot

Head

Attach handle

Shell Side (D)
77 holes x 30 holes
Cut 2, reverse 1

Foot

COLOR KEY	
Yards	**Plastic Canvas Yarn**
10 (9.2m)	☐ Lemon #235
106 (97m)	☐ Buff #334
75 (68.6m)	■ Tea leaf #624
	∕ Lemon #235 Running Stitch
	∕ Buff #334 Running Stitch
	6-Strand Embroidery Floss
12 (11m)	∕ Green Running Stitch

Color numbers given are for Red Heart Super Saver Art. E300 medium weight yarn.

Harness (E)
11 holes x 5 holes
Cut 1

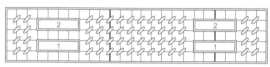

Shoulder Strap Brace (F)
25 holes x 5 holes
Cut 1

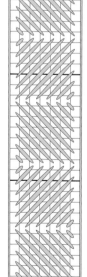

Continue pattern

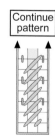

Continue pattern

Hood Band (I)
3 holes x 145 holes
Cut 2

Hood Band (J)
3 holes x 141 holes
Cut 2

Buckle & Buckle Brace (G)
5 holes x 7 holes
Cut 2

Handle (H)
7 holes x 150 holes
Cut 2

5-Inch Doll Cradle

Size: 6½ inches W x 7½ inches L x 5⅛ inches H
(15.2cm x 19cm x 13cm)
Skill Level: Advanced

Materials
- ❏ 1 artist-style sheet clear 7-count plastic canvas
- ❏ 1 regular-size sheet clear 7-count plastic canvas
- ❏ Red Heart Super Saver Art. E300 medium weight yarn as listed in color key
- ❏ #16 tapestry needle
- ❏ Stuffing material (sample used small flat pieces of plastic foam)

Project Note
Follow graphs and assembly diagram throughout.

Cutting & Stitching

1 Cut plastic canvas according to graphs (pages 26–29), cutting out holes on sides (A), outer headboard and footboard (B) pieces and inner headboard and footboard (C) pieces where indicated. Mattress base (F) will remain unstitched.

2 Stitch remaining pieces following graphs.

Assembly

1 Use buff yarn throughout assembly. With wrong sides together, Whipstitch cutout edges of two sides (A) together, then Whipstitch top edges together. Repeat with remaining two side (A) pieces. Set aside.

2 Whipstitch one rocker (E) to each outer headboard and footboard (B) from arrow to arrow, easing as necessary to fit. Whipstitch top edges of inner rocker sides (D) to mattress base (F) where indicated with red lines, making sure wrong sides are facing rocker sides on outer headboard and footboard (B) pieces.

3 Place wrong sides of mattress pieces (F and G) together with mattress quilt (G) on top and inner rocker sides (D) on bottom. With right sides facing, Whipstitch short edges to bottom edges of inner headboard and footboard (C) pieces, working through all three thicknesses.

4 Matching top edges and with wrong sides together, Whipstitch cutout edges of one outer headboard and footboard (B) and one inner headboard and footboard (C) together, then Whipstitch top edges together. Repeat with remaining outer headboard (B) and inner headboard (C).

5 Whipstitch side edges of sides (A) and headboard and footboard pieces (B and C) together from blue dots to arrows, working through all four thicknesses and Whipstitching corners of mattresses (F and G) to headboard and footboard pieces (B and C) at bottom of sides (A).

6 Whipstitch bottom edges of sides (A) to mattress pieces (F and G) between rockers, working through all four thicknesses.

7 Place stuffing material between rocker sides. *Note: Cut to fit if using flat plastic foam.* Whipstitch rockers (E) to inner rocker sides (D), easing as necessary to fit. Whipstitch short edges of rockers (E) to remaining bottom edges of mattresses (F and G).

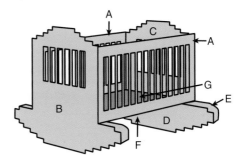

5-Inch Doll Cradle
Assembly Diagram

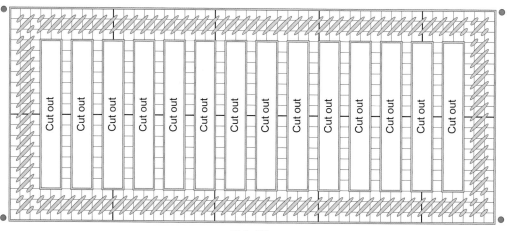

Side (A)
47 holes x 20 holes
Cut 4

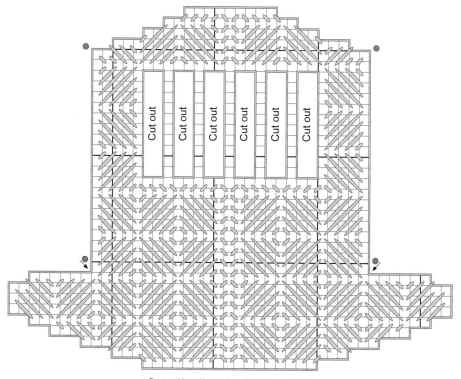

Outer Headboard & Footboard (B)
43 holes x 34 holes
Cut 2

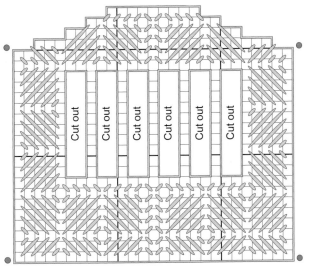

Inner Headboard & Footboard (C)
27 holes x 24 holes
Cut 2

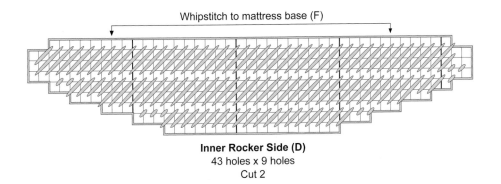

Inner Rocker Side (D)
43 holes x 9 holes
Cut 2

COLOR KEY

Yards	Plastic Canvas Yarn
15 (13.8m)	☐ Lemon #235
156 (142.7m)	☐ Buff #334
10 (9.2m)	■ Tea leaf #624

Color numbers given are for Red Heart Super Saver Art. E300 medium weight yarn.

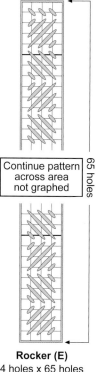

Continue pattern across area not graphed

65 holes

Rocker (E)
4 holes x 65 holes
Cut 2

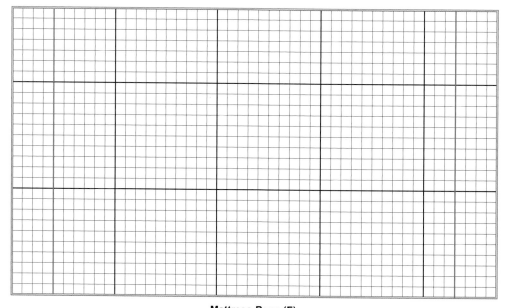

Mattress Base (F)
47 holes x 27 holes
Cut 1
Do not stitch

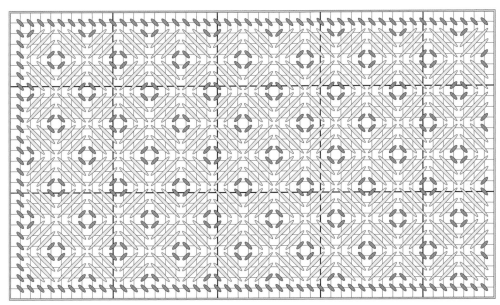

Mattress Quilt (G)
47 holes x 27 holes
Cut 1

10-Inch Doll Cradle

Size: 11⅜ inches W x 12 inches L x 9½ inches H
(28.9cm x 30.5cm x 24.1cm)
Skill Level: Advanced

Materials

- ❏ 4 artist-style sheets clear 7-count plastic canvas
- ❏ Red Heart Super Saver Art. E300 medium weight yarn as listed in color key
- ❏ #16 tapestry needle
- ❏ 2 (11-inch/27.9cm) lengths 5mm dowels
- ❏ Stuffing material (sample used plastic foam packing peanuts)

Project Note

Follow graphs and assembly diagram throughout.

Cutting & Stitching

1 Cut plastic canvas according to graphs (pages 31–37), cutting out holes on sides (A), outer headboard and footboard (B) pieces and inner headboard and footboard (C) pieces where indicated. Mattress base (F) will remain unstitched.

2 Stitch remaining pieces following graphs.

Assembly

1 Use buff yarn throughout assembly. With wrong sides together, Whipstitch cutout edges of two sides (A) together. Insert one dowel between sides (A) at top, then Whipstitch side and top edges together from blue dot to blue dot. Repeat with remaining two side (A) pieces and dowel. Set aside.

2 Whipstitch one rocker (E) to each outer headboard and footboard (B) from arrow to arrow, easing as necessary to fit. Whipstitch top edges of inner rocker sides (D) to mattress base (F) where indicated with red lines, making sure wrong sides are facing rocker sides on outer headboard and footboard (B) pieces.

3 Place wrong sides of mattress pieces (F and G) together with mattress quilt (G) on top and inner rocker sides (D) on bottom. With right sides facing, Whipstitch short edges of quilt pieces (F and G) to bottom edges of inner headboard and footboard (C) pieces, working through all three thicknesses.

4 Matching top edges and with wrong sides together, Whipstitch cutout edges of one outer headboard and footboard (B) and one inner headboard and footboard (C) together, then Whipstitch top edges together. Repeat with remaining outer headboard (B) and inner headboard (C).

5 Whipstitch side edges of sides (A) and headboard and footboard pieces (B and C) together from blue dot to blue dot, working through all four thicknesses and Whipstitching corners of mattresses (F and G) to headboard and footboard pieces (B and C) at bottom of sides (A).

6 Whipstitch bottom edges of sides (A) to mattress pieces (F and G) between rockers, working through all four thicknesses.

7 Whipstitch rockers (E) to inner rocker sides (D), easing as necessary to fit and filling with stuffing material before closing. Whipstitch short edges of rockers (E) to remaining bottom edges of mattresses (F and G).

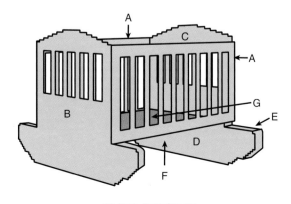

10-Inch Doll Cradle
Assembly Diagram

COLOR KEY

Yards	Plastic Canvas Yarn
20 (18.3m)	☐ Lemon #235
260 (238m)	☐ Buff #334
30 (27.5m)	■ Tea leaf #624

Color numbers given are for Red Heart Super Saver Art. E300 medium weight yarn.

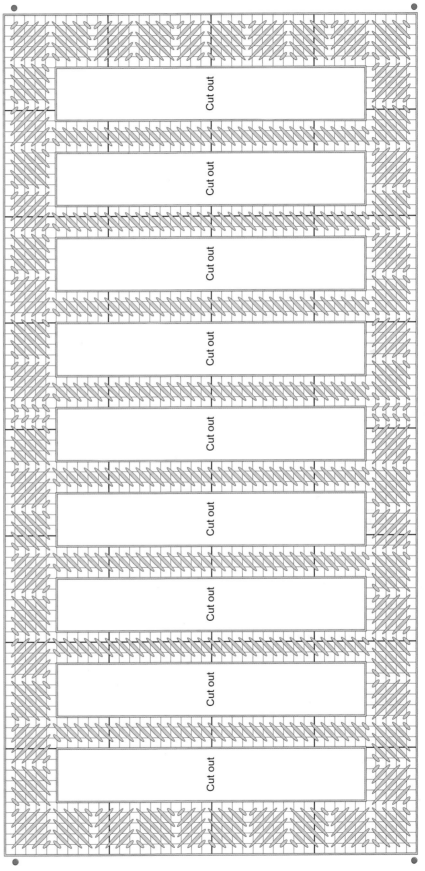

Side (A)
79 holes x 40 holes
Cut 4

Cut out

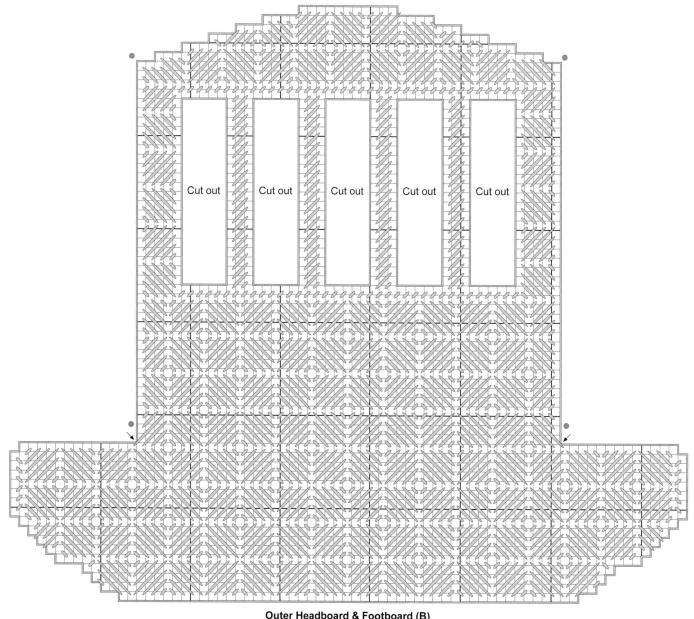

Outer Headboard & Footboard (B)
75 holes x 64 holes
Cut 2

Cut out Cut out Cut out Cut out Cut out

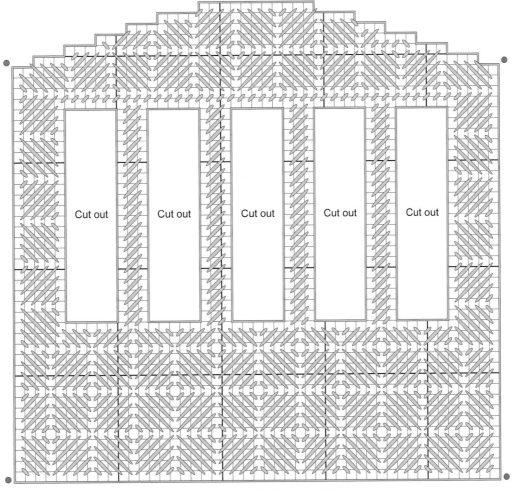

Inner Headboard & Footboard (C)
47 holes x 45 holes
Cut 2

Whipstitch to mattress base (F)

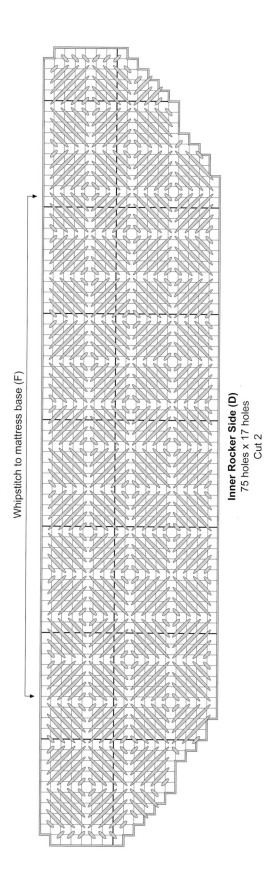

Inner Rocker Side (D)
75 holes x 17 holes
Cut 2

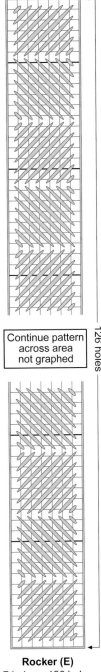

Continue pattern
across area
not graphed

126 holes

Rocker (E)
7 holes x 126 holes
Cut 2

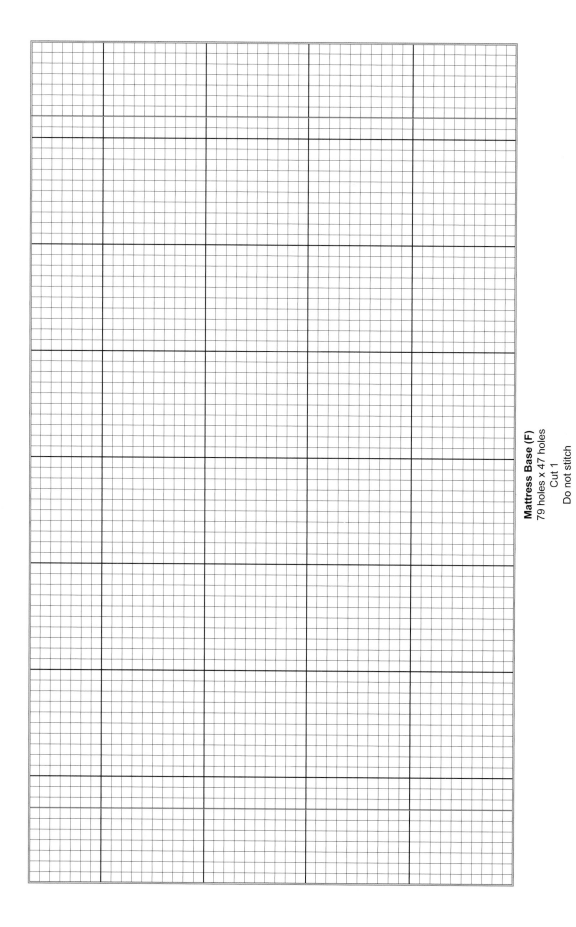

Mattress Base (F)
79 holes x 47 holes
Cut 1
Do not stitch

COLOR KEY

Yards	Plastic Canvas Yarn
20 (18.3m)	☐ Lemon #235
260 (238m)	☐ Buff #334
30 (27.5m)	■ Tea leaf #624

Color numbers given are for Red Heart Super Saver Art. E300 medium weight yarn.

Mattress Quilt (G)
79 holes x 47 holes
Cut 1

5-Inch Doll Stroller

Size: 5¾ inches W x 8 inches L x 7½ inches H
(14.6cm x 20.3cm x 19cm)
Skill Level: Advanced

Materials
- ❏ 1 artist-style sheet clear 7-count plastic canvas
- ❏ Small amount ivory 7-count plastic canvas
- ❏ Red Heart Super Saver Art. E300 medium weight yarn as listed in color key
- ❏ #16 tapestry needle
- ❏ 17 inches (43.2cm) ½-inch/12mm-wide brown grosgrain ribbon
- ❏ ¾ inch (1.9cm) ½-inch/1.3cm-wide hook-and-loop tape
- ❏ 8 (1½-inch/38mm) wooden wheels
- ❏ 5mm wooden dowels:
    2 (3½-inch/8.9cm) lengths
    2 (5½-inch/14cm) lengths
    2 (6-inch/15.2cm) lengths
- ❏ Craft paint: black, silver
- ❏ Small paintbrush
- ❏ Glossy sealer
- ❏ 4 small flat metal washers with opening to fit 5mm wooden dowel (outer diameter no larger than ⅝ inch/1.6cm)
- ❏ Hand-sewing needle
- ❏ Heavy carpet thread
- ❏ Craft glue

Project Note
Follow graphs and assembly diagrams throughout.

Painting, Cutting, Stitching

1 Paint wheels black and centers of wheels silver. Paint 5½-inch/14cm-long dowels silver; paint ends black. Allow to dry.

2 When dry, apply glossy sealer to wheels and dowels. Allow to dry.

3 Cut harness (F), shoulder strap brace (G) and buckle and buckle brace (H) from ivory plastic canvas according to graphs (page 42), cutting out holes where indicated. These pieces will remain unstitched.

4 Cut remaining pieces from clear plastic canvas according to graphs (pages 40–42), cutting out holes on seat front (A), back legs (D) and front legs/handle (E) where indicated.

5 Stitch pieces following graphs, leaving yellow shaded areas on back legs (D) and front legs/handle (E) unstitched.

6 Overcast cutout holes on seat front (A) with Aspen print.

Seat Belt Assembly

1 Cut ribbon into one 5½-inch (14cm) length and one 11½-inch (29.2cm) length.

2 For shoulder straps, thread ends of 11½-inch (29.2cm) length of ribbon up through holes 1 on harness (F) and down through holes 2. Pull ribbon through, leaving about a 1-inch (2.5cm) loop.

3 Thread ends through two shoulder strap holes near head edge of seat front (A). Place shoulder strap brace (G) behind shoulder strap holes on seat front (A) and thread through holes 1 and 2 following step 2. Pull ribbon through, measuring with doll for correct fit and making sure to leave enough room for doll's head to fit.

4 Using hand-sewing needle and carpet thread, sew ribbon to shoulder strap brace (G), trimming ends as needed. Sew brace (G) to back of seat front (A).

5 For adjuster strap, thread one end of 5½-inch (14cm) length of ribbon through buckle brace (H), coming up through hole 1 and going down through hole 2; sew ribbon in place to buckle brace (H) and to back seat front (A).

6 Thread other end of ribbon up through bottom hole of seat front (A), then up through hole 1 of buckle (H) and down through hole 2. Fold ribbon down on back side of buckle (H) and sew to one side of hook-and-loop tape and to buckle (H), trimming as needed. Sew other side of hook-and-loop tape to seat front (A) where indicated with pink shading.

7 To fasten, bring adjuster strap up through loop below harness on shoulder straps and fasten hook-and-loop tape pieces together.

Legs Assembly

1 Use tea green yarn throughout legs assembly. With wrong sides together, Whipstitch two back legs (A) together along one long side.

2 Lay open with wrong sides faceup. Apply a line of glue along center of one back leg (D) and insert one 3½-inch (8.9cm) dowel. *Note: Do not apply glue to unstitched areas and make sure glue does not spread to holes along Whipstitch edges.* Whipstitch down remaining long side to bottom end, insert one metal washer where indicated, then Whipstitch around bottom end.

3 Repeat with remaining back legs (D).

4 With wrong sides together, Whipstitch front legs/handle (E) together along one long edge on each end between blue dots. Lay open with wrong sides faceup. Apply a 6-inch (15.2cm) line of glue along center of one front leg (E) at both ends, beginning at stitch lines. *Note: Do not apply glue to unstitched areas and make sure glue does not spread to holes along Whipstitch edges.*

5 Insert 6-inch (15.2cm) dowels along glue lines. Before glue dries, follow Fig. 1 and insert one assembled back leg (D) between legs/handle (E). Whipstitch together along all remaining edges, inserting metal washer in both ends and working through all four thicknesses where back legs (D) are inserted.

Seat Assembly

1 Use tea green throughout seat assembly. With wrong sides together, Whipstitch top edges of seat front and back (A and B) together around side and top edges from blue dot to blue dot. Whipstitch bottom edges together. Set aside.

2 With wrong sides of one inner seat side (C1) and outer seat side (C2) together, Whipstitch along edges indicated within brackets. Repeat with remaining inner and outer seat sides (C1 and C2).

3 Whipstitch sides to seat from blue dot to red dot, working through all four thicknesses.

Final Assembly

1 Use tea green throughout. Placing one back leg (D), on one outer seat side (C2) where indicated with red lines and keeping front edges of seat sides even with edges of front leg/handle (E), securely tack legs and sides together. Repeat with remaining legs and side.

2 Insert end of one painted dowel from outside to inside through end of one front leg/handle (E) and metal washer. Thread on two wheels, then insert end from inside to outside on opposite side of leg through metal washer.

3 Using photo as a guide, thread on two outer wheels and glue in place to dowel. Glue inner wheels in place to dowel. *Note: Before gluing, make sure inside of each wheel is facing front leg.*

4 Repeat steps 2 and 3 for back wheels.

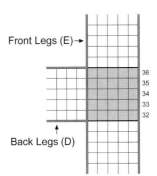

Fig. 1
Place back legs (D)
between front legs (E)
at holes 32–36

Front Legs (E) →

Back Legs (D)

36
35
34
33
32

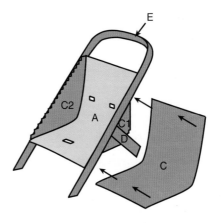

5-Inch Doll Stroller
Assembly Diagram

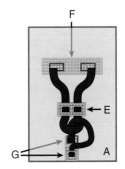

5-Inch Doll Stroller
Seat Belt Assembly Diagram

Seat Front (A)
25 holes x 37 holes
Cut 1 from clear

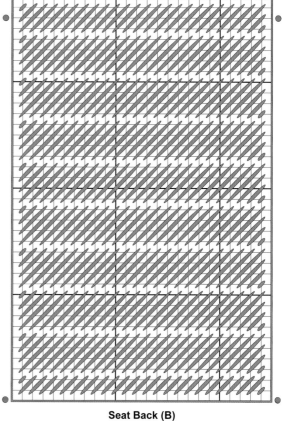

Seat Back (B)
25 holes x 38 holes
Cut 1 from clear

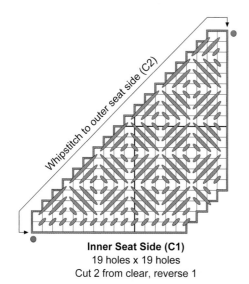

Whipstitch to outer seat side (C2)

Inner Seat Side (C1)
19 holes x 19 holes
Cut 2 from clear, reverse 1

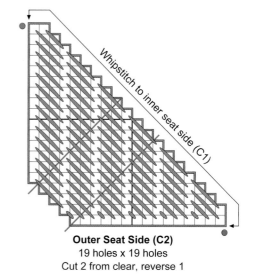

Whipstitch to inner seat side (C1)

Outer Seat Side (C2)
19 holes x 19 holes
Cut 2 from clear, reverse 1

COLOR KEY

Yards	Plastic Canvas Yarn
10 (9.2m)	☐ Aspen print #305
65 (59.5m)	■ Tea leaf #624
	◎ Attach metal washer

Color numbers given are for Red Heart Super Saver Art. E300 medium weight yarn.

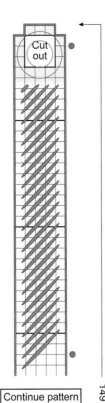

Continue pattern across area not graphed

149 holes

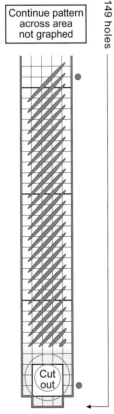

Insert between front legs/handle (E)

Cut out

Back Legs (D)
5 holes x 35 holes
Cut 4 from clear

Cut out

Cut out

Front Legs/Handle (E)
5 holes x 149 holes
Cut 2 from clear

Harness (F)
9 holes x 5 holes
Cut 1 from ivory
Do not stitch

Shoulder Strap Brace (G)
17 holes x 5 holes
Cut 1 from ivory
Do not stitch

Buckle & Buckle Brace (H)
5 holes x 5 holes
Cut 2 from ivory
Do not stitch

10-Inch Doll Stroller

Size: 8¾ inches W x 13 inches L x 11¾ inches H
(22.2cm x 33cm x 29.8cm)
Skill Level: Advanced

Materials
- ❏ 2 artist-style sheets clear 7-count plastic canvas
- ❏ Small amount ivory 7-count plastic canvas
- ❏ Red Heart Super Saver Art. E300 medium weight yarn as listed in color key
- ❏ #16 tapestry needle
- ❏ 24 inches (61cm) ½-inch/12mm-wide brown grosgrain ribbon
- ❏ ¾ inch (1.9cm) ½-inch/1.3cm-wide hook-and-loop tape
- ❏ 8 (2-inch/50.8mm) wooden wheels with ⅝-inch (1.6cm) holes
- ❏ 8mm wooden dowels:
    2 (8½-inch/21.6cm) lengths
    2 (12-inch/30.5cm) lengths
    2 (5-inch/12.7cm) lengths
- ❏ 2 (6-inch/15.2cm) lengths 4mm wooden dowels
- ❏ Craft paint: black, silver
- ❏ Small paintbrush
- ❏ Glossy sealer
- ❏ 4 (¾-inch/1.9cm) flat metal washers with ⁵⁄₁₆-inch (0.8cm) opening
- ❏ Hand-sewing needle
- ❏ Heavy carpet thread
- ❏ Craft glue

Project Note
Follow graphs and assembly diagrams throughout.

Painting, Cutting, Stitching

1 Paint wheels black and centers of wheels silver. Paint 8½-inch/21.6cm-long 8mm dowels silver; paint ends black. Allow to dry.

2 When dry, apply glossy sealer to wheels and dowels. Allow to dry.

3 Cut harness (F), shoulder strap brace (G) and buckle and buckle brace (H) from ivory plastic canvas according to graphs (page 49), cutting out holes where indicated. These pieces will remain unstitched.

4 Cut remaining pieces from clear plastic canvas according to graphs (pages 45–50), cutting out holes on seat front (A), back legs (D) and front legs (E) where indicated.

5 Stitch pieces following graphs, leaving yellow shaded areas on back legs (D) and front legs (E) unstitched. Reverse one inner seat side (C1) and one outer seat side (C2) before stitching.

6 Overcast cutout holes on seat front (A) with cornmeal and Aspen print.

Seat Belt Assembly

1 Cut ribbon into one 6-inch (15.2cm) length and one 18-inch (45.7cm) length.

2 For shoulder straps, thread ends of 18-inch (45.7cm) length ribbon up through holes 1 on harness (F) and down through holes 2. Pull ribbon through, leaving about a 3-inch (7.6cm) loop.

3 Thread ends through two shoulder strap holes near head edge of seat front (A). Place shoulder strap brace (G) behind shoulder strap holes on seat front (A) and thread through holes 1 and 2 following step 2. Pull ribbon through, measuring with doll for correct fit and making sure to leave enough room for doll's head to fit.

4 Using hand-sewing needle and carpet thread, sew ribbon to shoulder strap brace (G), trimming ends as needed. Sew brace (G) to back of seat front (A).

5 For adjuster strap, thread one end of 6-inch (15.2cm) length of ribbon through buckle brace (H), coming up through hole 1 and going down through hole 2; sew ribbon in place to buckle brace (H) and to back of seat front (A).

6 Thread other end of ribbon up through bottom hole of seat front (A), then up through hole 1 of buckle (H) and down through hole 2. Fold ribbon down on back side of buckle (H) and sew to one side of hook-and-loop tape and to buckle (H), trimming as needed. Sew other side of hook-and-loop tape to seat front (A) where indicated with pink shading.

7 To fasten, bring adjuster strap up through loop below harness on shoulder straps and fasten hook-and-loop tape pieces together.

Legs Assembly

1 Use tea green yarn throughout legs assembly. With wrong sides together, Whipstitch two back legs (A) together along one long side.

2 Lay open with wrong sides faceup. Apply a line of glue along center of one back leg (D) and insert one 5-inch(12.7cm) 8mm dowel. *Note: Do not apply glue to unstitched areas and make sure glue does not spread to holes along Whipstitch edges.* Whipstitch down remaining long side to bottom end, insert one metal washer where indicated, then Whipstitch around bottom end.

3 Repeat with remaining back legs (D).

4 With wrong sides together, Whipstitch two front legs (E) together along one long edge between brackets. Lay open with wrong sides faceup. Apply a 12-inch (30.5cm) line of glue along center of one front leg (E), beginning at stitch lines. *Note: Do not apply glue to unstitched areas and make sure glue does not spread to holes along Whipstitch edges.*

5 Insert a 12-inch (30.5cm) 8mm dowel along glue lines. Before glue dries, follow Fig. 1 and insert one assembled back leg (D) between front legs (E). Whipstitch together along remaining edges, leaving 5 holes unworked at top, inserting metal washer in bottom end where indicated and working through all four thicknesses where back leg (D) is inserted.

6 Repeat steps 4 and 5 with remaining legs.

Seat Assembly

1 Place wrong sides of seat front and back (A and B) together, and wrong sides of one seat front extension

(J) and one seat back extension (K) together at top and remaining seat front and back extensions (J and K) together at bottom. Whipstitch seats and extensions together with Aspen print, working through all four thicknesses.

2 Lay open top extension, apply a line of glue along center and insert one 6-inch (15.2cm) 4mm dowel. Whipstitch closed along remaining edges with tea green. Repeat with bottom extension.

3 With wrong sides of one inner seat side (C1) and outer seat side (C2) together, Whipstitch along top and front edges from blue dot to blue dot. Repeat with remaining inner and outer seat sides (C1 and C2).

4 Whipstitch remaining edges of sides to seat front (A) and seat back (B) from green dot to green dot, working through all four thicknesses.

Final Assembly

1 Use tea green throughout. Placing one back leg (D), on one outer seat side (C2) where indicated with red lines and keeping front edges of seat sides even with edges of front leg (E), securely tack legs to sides, assembled seat and extensions. Repeat with remaining legs and side.

2 Overcast ends of handles (I) from blue dot to blue dot. Whipstitch wrong sides together along long edges, leaving 5 holes unstitched on each end. Overlap 5 holes on ends with front legs; finish Whipstitching together, working through all four thicknesses.

3 Insert end of one painted dowel from outside to inside through end of one front leg (E) and metal washer. Thread on two wheels, then insert end from inside to outside through remaining leg and through metal washer.

4 Using photo as a guide, thread on two outer wheels and glue in place to dowel. Glue inner wheels in place to dowel. *Note: Before gluing, make sure inside of each wheel is facing front leg.*

5 Repeat steps 3 and 4 for back wheels.

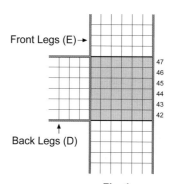

Fig. 1
Place back legs (D)
between front legs (E)
at holes 42—47

COLOR KEY

Yards	Plastic Canvas Yarn
60 (54.9m)	Aspen print #305
40 (36.6m)	Cornmeal #320
150 (137.2m)	Tea leaf #624
	Attach metal washer

Color numbers given are for Red Heart Super Saver Art. E300 medium weight yarn.

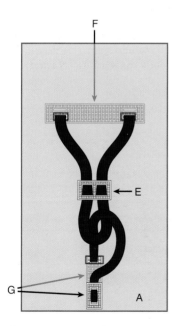

10-Inch Doll Stroller
Assembly Diagram

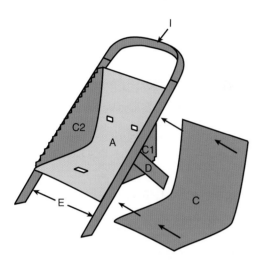

10-Inch Doll Stroller
Seat Belt Assembly Diagram

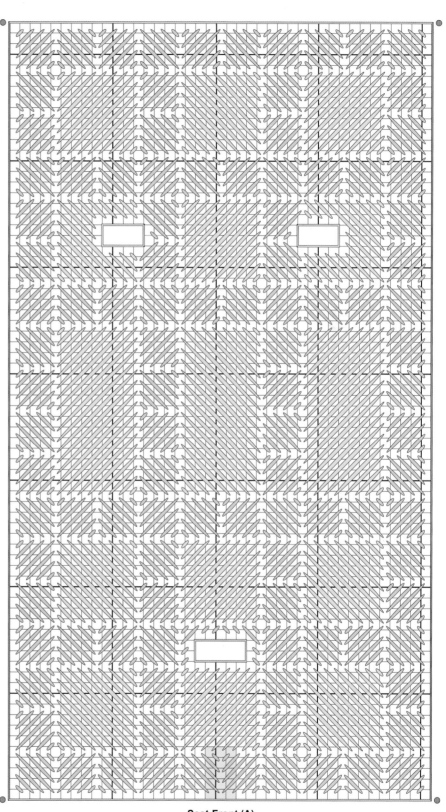

Seat Front (A)
41 holes x 73 holes
Cut 1 from clear

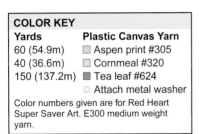

COLOR KEY

Yards	Plastic Canvas Yarn
60 (54.9m)	☐ Aspen print #305
40 (36.6m)	☐ Cornmeal #320
150 (137.2m)	▨ Tea leaf #624
	◎ Attach metal washer

Color numbers given are for Red Heart Super Saver Art. E300 medium weight yarn.

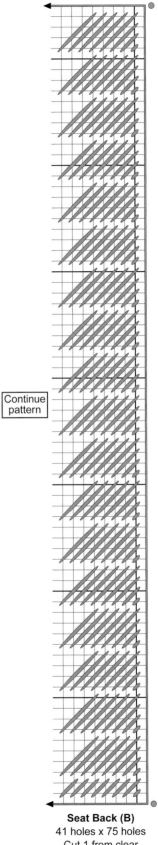

Continue pattern

Seat Back (B)
41 holes x 75 holes
Cut 1 from clear

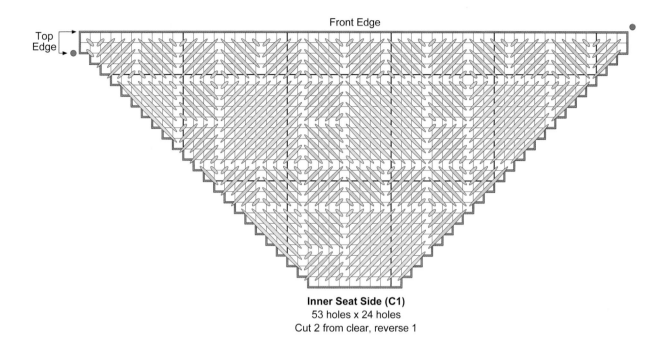

Front Edge

Top Edge

Inner Seat Side (C1)
53 holes x 24 holes
Cut 2 from clear, reverse 1

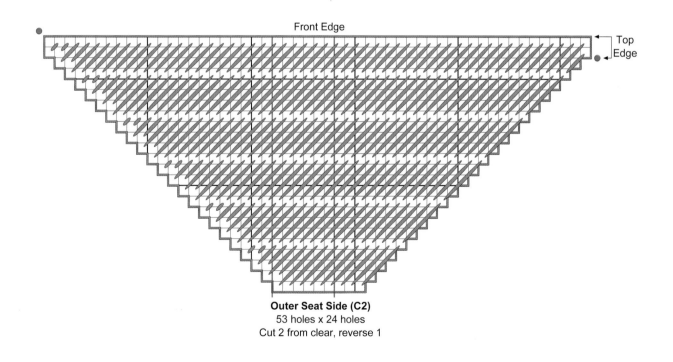

Front Edge

Top Edge

Outer Seat Side (C2)
53 holes x 24 holes
Cut 2 from clear, reverse 1

COLOR KEY

Yards	Plastic Canvas Yarn
60 (54.9m)	▨ Aspen print #305
40 (36.6m)	▢ Cornmeal #320
150 (137.2m)	▨ Tea leaf #624
	◎ Attach metal washer

Color numbers given are for Red Heart Super Saver Art. E300 medium weight yarn.

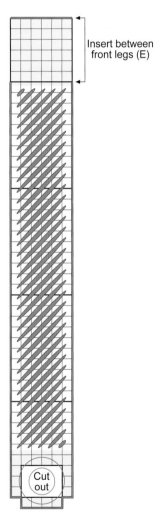

Insert between front legs (E)

Back Leg (D)
6 holes x 46 holes
Cut 4 from clear

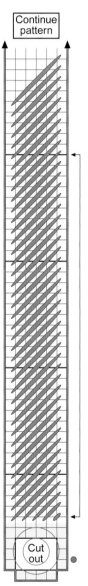

Continue pattern

Front Leg (E)
6 holes x 87 holes
Cut 4 from clear

Harness (F)
9 holes x 5 holes
Cut 1 from ivory
Do not stitch

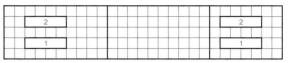

Shoulder Strap Brace (G)
27 holes x 5 holes
Cut 1 from ivory
Do not stitch

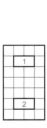

Buckle & Buckle Brace (H)
4 holes x 7 holes
Cut 2 from ivory
Do not stitch

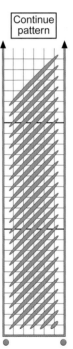

Continue
pattern

Handle (I)
6 holes x 73 holes
Cut 2 from clear

COLOR KEY	
Yards	**Plastic Canvas Yarn**
60 (54.9m)	▢ Aspen print #305
40 (36.6m)	▢ Cornmeal #320
150 (137.2m)	■ Tea leaf #624
	◎ Attach metal washer
Color numbers given are for Red Heart Super Saver Art. E300 medium weight yarn.	

Seat Front Extension (J)
43 holes x 4 holes
Cut 2 from clear

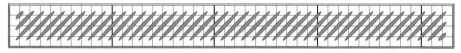

Seat Back Extension (K)
43 holes x 4 holes
Cut 1 from clear

5-Inch Doll High Chair

Size: 5¾ inches W x 7½ inches H x 8 inches D
(14.6cm x 19cm x 20.3cm)
Skill Level: Advanced

Materials

❏ 1 artist-style sheet 7-count plastic canvas
❏ Red Heart Super Saver Art. E300 medium weight
   yarn as listed in color key
❏ #16 tapestry needle
❏ 2 (¾ inch/1.9cm) lengths ½-inch/1.3cm-wide hook-
   and-loop tape
❏ Hand-sewing needle
❏ Heavy carpet thread

Project Note

Follow graphs and assembly diagram throughout.

Cutting & Stitching

1 Cut plastic canvas according to graphs (pages 52–55), cutting out holes in outer chair back (A), inner back legs (C), outer chair sides (D), inner side legs (E) and front legs (H). Cut one 90-hole x 1-hole piece for tray side (J).

2 Seat bottom (G) and tray side (J) will remain unstitched. Stitch remaining pieces following graphs.

Chair Assembly

1 Using tea leaf, and with right sides facing in throughout, Whipstitch inner chair sides (F) to side edges of stitched seat (G), easing as necessary to fit. Whipstitch back edge of seat (G) to bottom edge of inner chair back (B). Whipstitch inner chair sides (F) to inner chair back (B) from green dot to red dot.

2 Using buff and with right sides facing in throughout, Whipstitch top edges of inner side legs (E) to side edges of unstitched seat bottom (G), easing as necessary to fit. Whipstitch top edges of inner back legs (C) to back edge of unstitched seat bottom (G).

3 With wrong sides facing, Whipstitch outer chair back (A) to outer chair sides (D) from green dots to red dots.

4 Slip assembled inner legs and unstitched seat (from step 2) inside assembled outer chair pieces (from step 3). Whipstitch inner back legs (C) to legs on outer chair back (A) around cutout edges and along bottom edges from blue dot to blue dot. Repeat with inner side legs (E) and legs on outer chair sides (D).

5 Slip assembled inner chair sides and stitched seat into top part of assembled chair. Using tea green, Whipstitch front edges of outer chair sides (D) and inner chair sides (F) together from green dots to red dots.

6 Whipstitch outer chair back (A) to inner chair back (B) around side and top edges from green dot to green dot.

7 Whipstitch back and side legs together along corners, working through all four thicknesses.

8 With wrong sides facing, Whipstitch front legs (H) together around cutout edges and along bottom edges from blue dot to blue dot. Whipstitch top edges to both seat (G) front edges, attaching leg divider where indicated while Whipstitching. Whipstitch side and front legs together at corners, working through all four thicknesses.

9 Whipstitch top edges of chair sides together, attaching tray rest (J) to both sides from yellow star to yellow star while Whipstitching. Overcast remaining edges of tray rest (K), attaching leg divider (L) to front edge of tray rest (K) where indicated while Overcasting.

Tray Assembly

1 Using hand-sewing needle and carpet thread, attach one side of each length of hook-and-loop tape to tray rest (K) where indicated with blue shading, cutting tape to fit before stitching. Sew remaining sides of hook and loop tape to right side of tray bottom (I) where indicated with blue shading.

2 Beginning on an inside edge, Whipstitch tray side (J) to tray top and bottom (I), easing as necessary to fit and overlapping ends as needed. Place tray on tray rest, securing with hoop-and-loop tape.

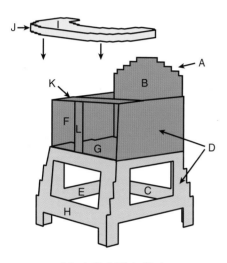

5-Inch Doll High Chair
Assembly Diagram

COLOR KEY	
Yards	**Plastic Canvas Yarn**
20 (18.3m)	☐ Lemon #235
75 (68.6m)	☐ Buff #334
75 (68.6m)	☐ Tea leaf #624
Color numbers given are for Red Heart Super Saver Art. E300 medium weight yarn.	

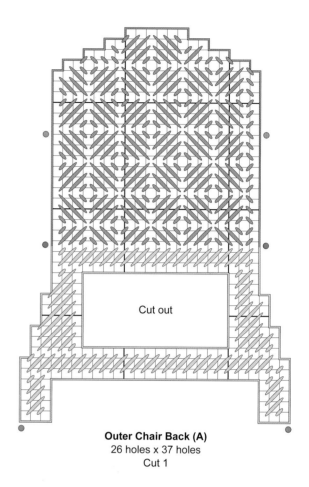

Outer Chair Back (A)
26 holes x 37 holes
Cut 1

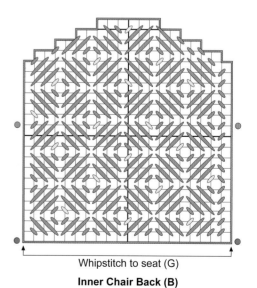

Whipstitch to seat (G)

Inner Chair Back (B)
20 holes x 21 holes
Cut 1

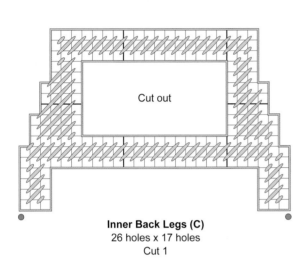

Inner Back Legs (C)
26 holes x 17 holes
Cut 1

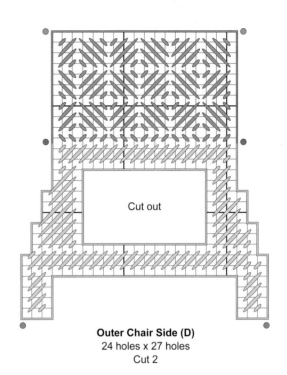

Outer Chair Side (D)
24 holes x 27 holes
Cut 2

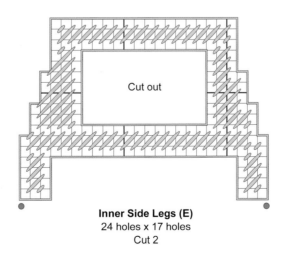

Inner Side Legs (E)
24 holes x 17 holes
Cut 2

COLOR KEY

Yards	Plastic Canvas Yarn
20 (18.3m)	☐ Lemon #235
75 (68.6m)	☐ Buff #334
75 (68.6m)	■ Tea leaf #624

Color numbers given are for Red Heart Super Saver Art. E300 medium weight yarn.

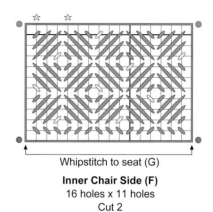

Whipstitch to seat (G)

Inner Chair Side (F)
16 holes x 11 holes
Cut 2

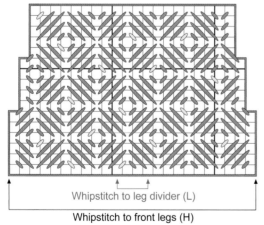

Whipstitch to leg divider (L)

Whipstitch to front legs (H)

Seat Top & Bottom (G)
24 holes x 16 holes
Cut 2
Stitch top only

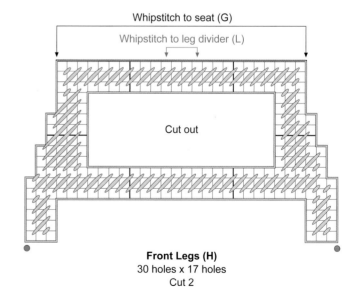

Whipstitch to seat (G)

Whipstitch to leg divider (L)

Cut out

Front Legs (H)
30 holes x 17 holes
Cut 2

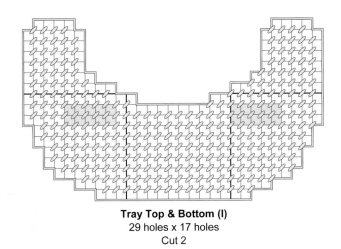

Tray Top & Bottom (I)
29 holes x 17 holes
Cut 2

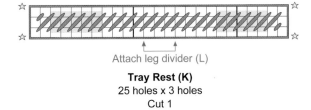

Attach leg divider (L)

Tray Rest (K)
25 holes x 3 holes
Cut 1

Leg Divider (L)
3 holes x 11 holes
Cut 1

10-Inch Doll High Chair

Size: 10½ inches W x 10¼ inches H x 9¼ inches D
(26.7cm x 26cm x 23.5cm)
Skill Level: Advanced

Materials

- ❏ 3 artist-style sheets 7-count plastic canvas
- ❏ Red Heart Super Saver Art. E300 medium weight yarn as listed in color key
- ❏ #16 tapestry needle
- ❏ 4mm wooden dowels
  8 (6-inch/15.2cm) lengths
  2 (5-inch/12.7cm) lengths
- ❏ 4 inches (10.2cm) ¾-inch/1.9cm-wide hook-and-loop tape
- ❏ Hand-sewing needle
- ❏ Heavy carpet thread

Project Note

Follow graphs and assembly diagram throughout.

Cutting & Stitching

1 Cut plastic canvas according to graphs (pages 58–63), cutting out holes in outer chair back (A), inner back legs (C), outer chair sides (D), inner side legs (E) and front legs (H).

2 Seat bottom (G) will remain unstitched. Stitch remaining pieces following graphs, reversing one inner chair side (F) before stitching.

Chair Assembly

1 Using tea leaf and with right sides facing in throughout, Whipstitch inner chair sides (F) to side edges of stitched seat top (G). Whipstitch back edge of seat top (G) to bottom edge of inner chair back (B). Whipstitch inner chair sides (F) to inner chair back (B) from green dot to red dot.

2 Using buff and with right sides facing in throughout, Whipstitch top edges of inner side legs (E) to side edges of unstitched seat bottom (G). Whipstitch top edges of inner back legs (C) to back edge of unstitched seat bottom (G).

3 With wrong sides facing, Whipstitch outer chair back (A) to outer chair sides (D) from green dots to red dots, Overcasting remaining hole at top of outer chair sides (D).

4 Slip assembled inner legs and unstitched seat (from step 2) inside assembled outer chair pieces (from step 3). Whipstitch inner back legs (C) to legs on outer chair back (A) around cutout edges and along bottom edges from blue dot to blue dot. Insert 6-inch (15.2cm) dowels where indicated with blue shading before closing. Work a Running Stitch (page 57) between two top rows of buff stitches where indicated.

5 Repeat with inner side legs (E) and legs on outer chair sides (D), also inserting 5-inch (12.7cm) dowel where indicated with pink shading before closing.

6 Slip assembled inner chair pieces into top part of assembled chair. Using tea green, Whipstitch front edges of outer chair sides (D) and inner chair sides (F) together from green dots to red dots.

7 Whipstitch outer chair back (A) to inner chair back (B) around side and top edges from green dot to green dot.

8 Whipstitch back and side legs together along corners, working through all four thicknesses.

9 With wrong sides facing, Whipstitch front legs (H) together around cutout edges and along bottom edges from blue dot to blue dot, inserting 6-inch (15.2cm) dowels where indicated with blue shading before closing.

10 Overcast side edges of leg dividers (L) where indicated from blue dot to blue dot. With wrong sides facing, Whipstitch remaining side edges together from blue dots to bottom edge.

11 Whipstitch top edges of front legs (H) to seat top and bottom (G), attaching bottom edge of leg divider (L) where indicated while Whipstitching. Whipstitch side and front legs together at corners, working through all four thicknesses.

Tray & Tray Rest Assembly

1 Using hand-sewing needle and carpet thread, sew one side of hook-and-loop tape to one tray rest (K) where indicated with peach shading. Sew remaining side of hook-and-loop tape to right side of tray bottom (I) where indicated with peach shading.

2 With wrong sides facing, Whipstitch tray rest (K) pieces together along long edges, making sure piece with hook-and-loop tape is on top; while Whipstitching, attach one side of leg divider to one tray rest (K) edge where indicated and remaining side of leg divider (L) to other side of tray rest (K).

3 Whipstitch top edges of chair sides together, attaching tray rest (K) to both sides from yellow star to yellow star while Whipstitching, working through all four thicknesses.

4 Beginning on an inside edge, Whipstitch tray side (J) to tray top and bottom (I), easing as necessary to fit and overlapping ends as needed. Place tray on tray rest, securing with hook-and-loop tape.

Running Stitch

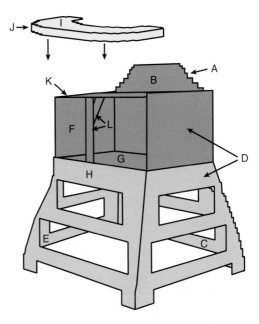

10-Inch Doll High Chair
Assembly Diagram

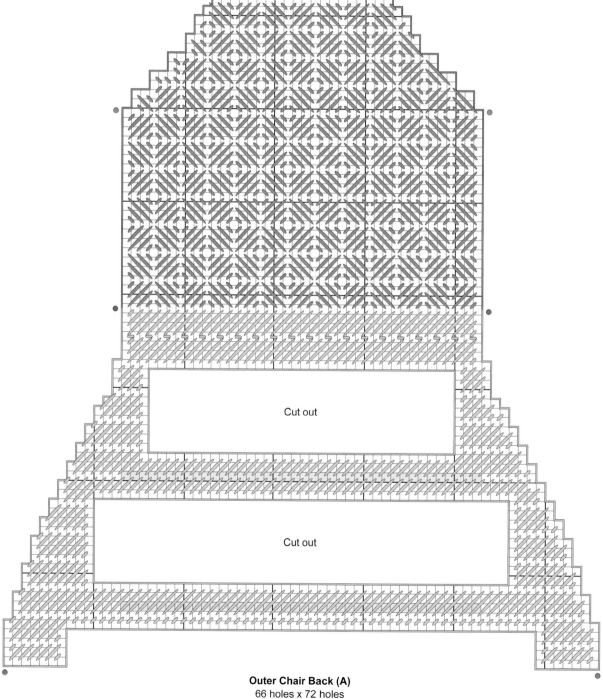

Outer Chair Back (A)
66 holes x 72 holes
Cut 1

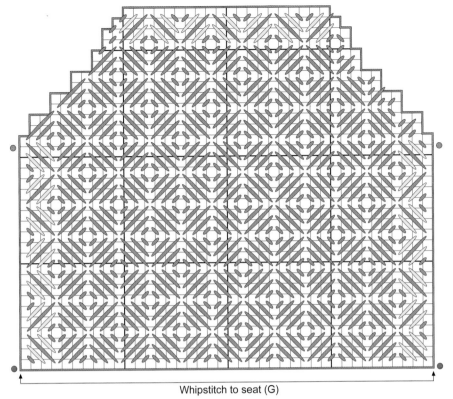

Whipstitch to seat (G)

Inner Chair Back (B)
40 holes x 34 holes
Cut 1

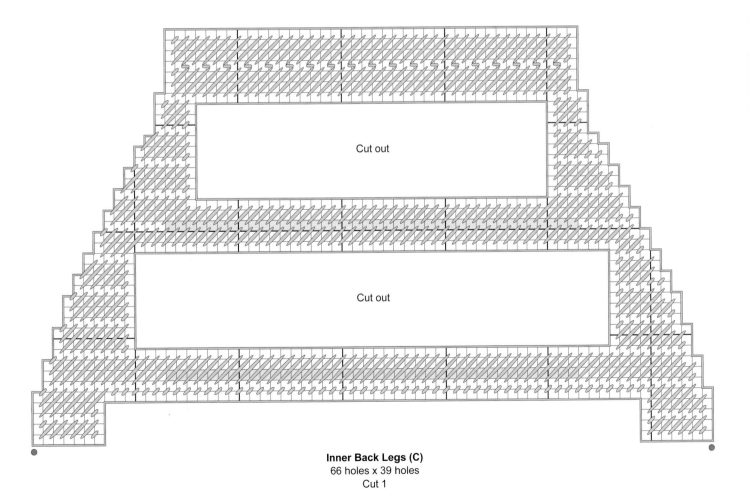

Cut out

Cut out

Inner Back Legs (C)
66 holes x 39 holes
Cut 1

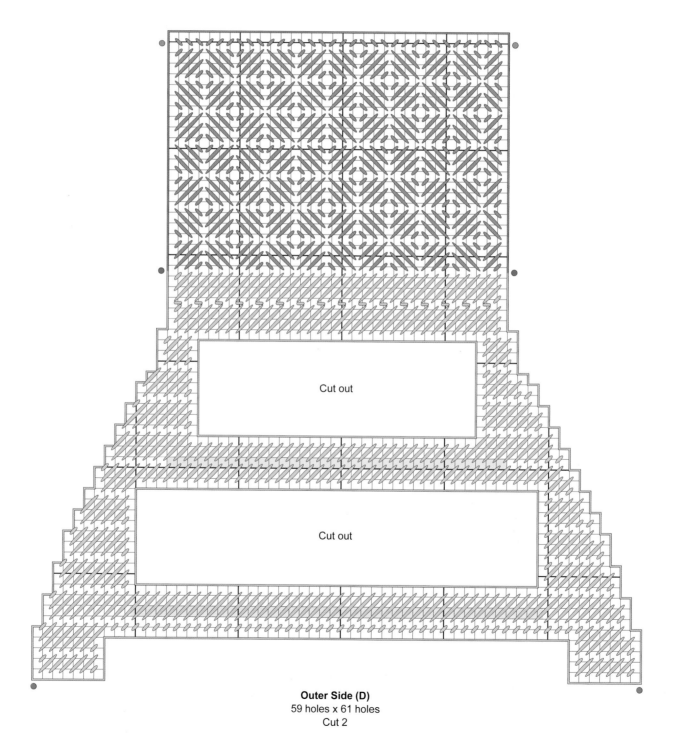

COLOR KEY

Yards	Plastic Canvas Yarn
52 (47.6m)	☐ Lemon #235
156 (142.7m)	☐ Buff #334
104 (95.1m)	■ Tea leaf #624
	╱ Buff #334 Running Stitch

Color numbers given are for Red Heart Super Saver Art. E300 medium weight yarn.

Cut out

Cut out

Outer Side (D)
59 holes x 61 holes
Cut 2

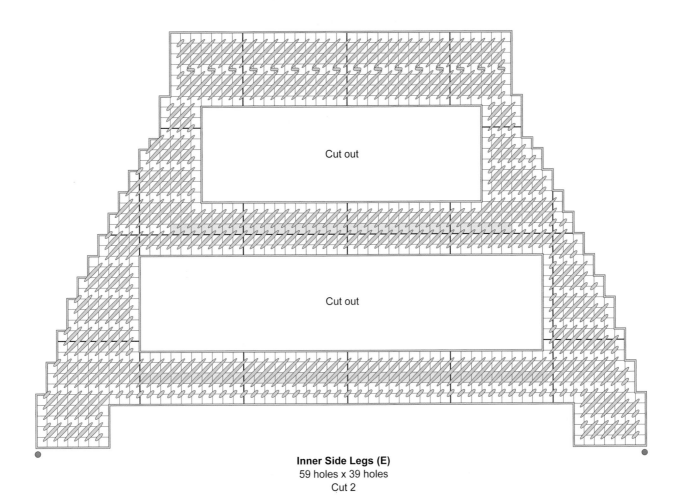

Inner Side Legs (E)
59 holes x 39 holes
Cut 2

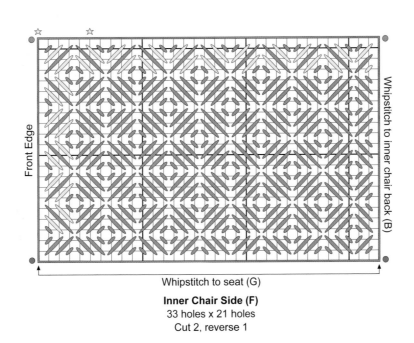

Front Edge

Whipstitch to inner chair back (B)

Whipstitch to seat (G)

Inner Chair Side (F)
33 holes x 21 holes
Cut 2, reverse 1

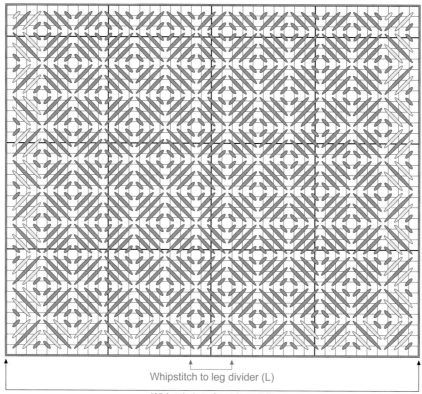

Whipstitch to leg divider (L)

Whipstitch to front legs (H)

Seat Top & Bottom (G)
40 holes x 33 holes
Cut 2
Stitch top only

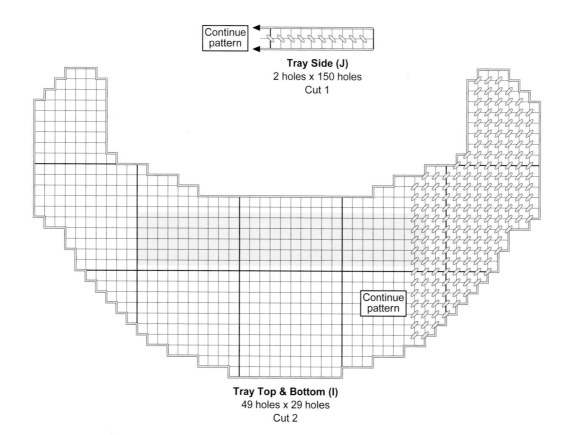

Continue pattern

Tray Side (J)
2 holes x 150 holes
Cut 1

Continue pattern

Tray Top & Bottom (I)
49 holes x 29 holes
Cut 2

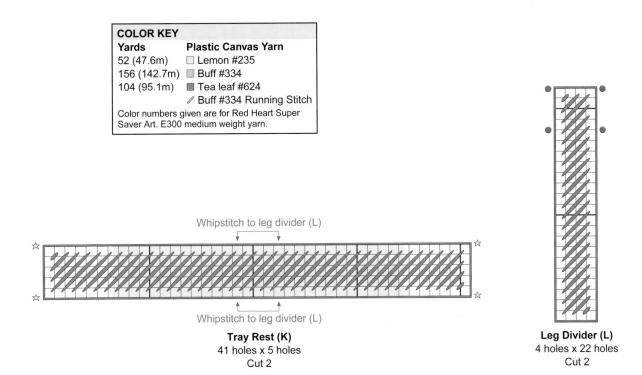

COLOR KEY

Yards	Plastic Canvas Yarn
52 (47.6m)	☐ Lemon #235
156 (142.7m)	☐ Buff #334
104 (95.1m)	■ Tea leaf #624
	╱ Buff #334 Running Stitch

Color numbers given are for Red Heart Super Saver Art. E300 medium weight yarn.

Whipstitch to leg divider (L)

Whipstitch to leg divider (L)

Tray Rest (K)
41 holes x 5 holes
Cut 2

Leg Divider (L)
4 holes x 22 holes
Cut 2

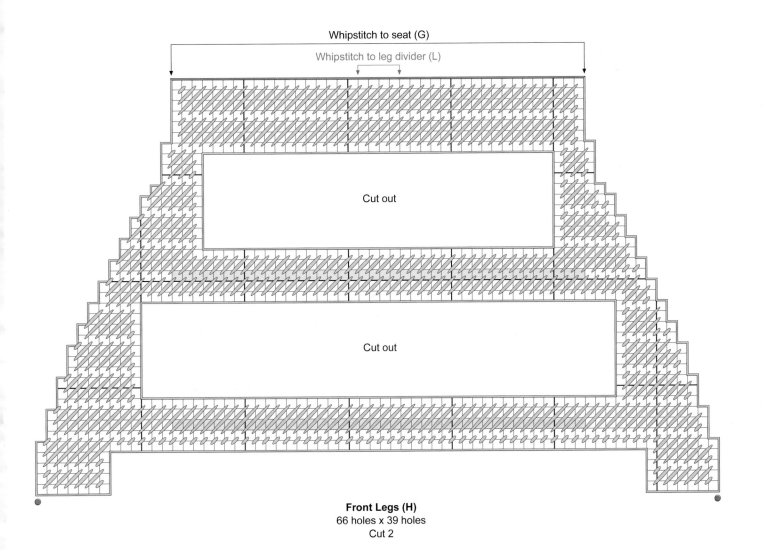

Whipstitch to seat (G)

Whipstitch to leg divider (L)

Cut out

Cut out

Front Legs (H)
66 holes x 39 holes
Cut 2

Getting Started

Before You Cut

Buy one brand of canvas for each entire project as brands can differ slightly in the distance between bars. Count holes carefully from the graph before you cut, using the bolder lines that show every 10 holes. These 10-count lines begin from the left side for vertical lines and from the bottom for horizontal lines. Mark canvas before cutting; then remove all marks completely before stitching. If the piece is cut in a rectangular or square shape and is either not worked, or worked with only one color and one type of stitch, the graph may not be included in the pattern. Instead, the cutting and stitching instructions are given in the general instructions or with the individual project instructions.

Covering the Canvas

Bring needle up from back of work, leaving a short length of yarn on back of canvas; work over short length to secure. To end a thread, weave needle and thread through the wrong side of your last few stitches; clip. Follow the numbers on the small graphs beside each stitch illustration; bring your needle up from the back of the work on odd numbers and down through the front of the work on even numbers. Work embroidery stitches last, after the canvas has been completely covered by the needlepoint stitches.

Shopping for Supplies

For supplies, first shop your local craft and needlework stores. Some supplies may be found in fabric, hardware and discount stores. If you are unable to find the supplies you need, please visit AnniesCatalog.com.

Basic Stitches
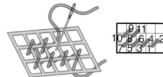

Continental
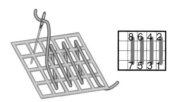

Cross

Long

Slanted Gobelin

Whipstitch

Overcast

Embroidery Stitches

Backstitch
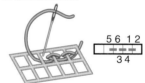

Lazy Daisy

Straight

French Knot

METRIC KEY:

millimeters = (mm)	meters = (m)
centimeters = (cm)	grams = (g)

Annie's™ *Furniture for 5- & 10-Inch Dolls* is published by Annie's, 306 East Parr Road, Berne, IN 46711. Printed in USA. Copyright © 2012 Annie's. All rights reserved. This publication may not be reproduced in part or in whole without written permission from the publisher.

RETAIL STORES: If you would like to carry this pattern book or any other Annie's publications, visit AnniesWSL.com

Every effort has been made to ensure that the instructions in this pattern book are complete and accurate. We cannot, however, take responsibility for human error, typographical mistakes or variations in individual work. Please visit AnniesCustomerCare.com to check for pattern updates.

ISBN: 978-1-59635-566-8
1 2 3 4 5 6 7 8 9